Rooftops of Tehran

Rooftops of Tehran

poems

SHOLEH WOLPÉ

RED HEN PRESS | Los Angeles, California

Rooftops of Tehran

Book design by Mark E. Cull

ISBN: 978-1-59709-110-7
Library of Congress Catalog Card Number: 2007943020

The City of Los Angeles Department of Cultural Affairs, Los Angeles County Arts Commission, California Arts Council and the National Endowment for the Arts partially support Red Hen Press.

First Edition

Published by Red Hen Press
www.redhen.org

For my aunts,
Ghamar, Shamsi, Guitty, Shaherzad, and Iren

And,
for my dear JWT

Acknowledgments

Iran is home to a beautiful ancient culture and a resilient, gracious people. United States is a country of men and women I deeply admire, and a government that in essence, and at its best, strives for justice, democracy and equality. Sometimes in crying out injustices, we do not often enough speak about human kindness, goodness and beauty—ever-present and everywhere . . . this is the thread that holds these dark poems together.

Many thanks go to my editor, Kate Gale, and publisher, Mark Cull, for their tireless efforts to represent diverse voices. In a world divided and darkened by prejudice and misunderstandings, literature can serve as a beacon of light facilitating constructive dialogue among those with opposing views. Small visionary presses like Red Hen Press help make this possible through publishing and supporting alternative views and voices.

I also thank and acknowledge the editors of the following journals and anthologies in which versions of these poems appeared:

Evensong: Contemporary Poems of Spirituality; Yellow as Turmeric, Fragrant as Cloves—An anthology of Asian American Female Poets; Inlandia: A Literary Journey Through California's Inland Empire; The Other Voices International Anthology; The Poetry of Iranian Women: A Contemporary Anthology; Di-verse-city, The Austin International Poetry Festival Anthology 2005; Poemeleon; The November 3rd Club; The Other Voices International; r.kv.r.y Quarterly Journal; Washington Square; Tupelo Press Poetry Project; ArteEast; Ash Canyon Review; and Exiled Ink.

A special thanks to Barrie Wexler for his wisdom, encouragement and kindness.

Contents

. . . To understand is continually to become, to see what only few can see and see it through the shifting sands of appearance as only you who fly can see.

—Farid UD-Din Attar
Conference of the Birds
Translated by: Raficq Abdullah

People are birds unable to fly.
—Mahmoud Darwish

Rooftop

Rooftop

Rooftops of my childhood were flat,
a place for sleeping on summer nights
on springy mattresses, under mosquito nets,
for grandmother's early calls to God,
for sister's secret rendezvous.

There I sought spirits among the twilight stars
but always my eyes heavy as stones—
or sin—
fell to
the street below

where a neighbor rushed home for his supper,
the salt seller pulled on his donkey's rein
or a servant girl hurried through, fresh bread under each arm.

On that rooftop I tasted my first kiss,
read *War and Peace* in Farsi, watched
the neighbor's teenage son decapitate
his sister's cat because his sister wouldn't wear
a headscarf to her classes at the university.

That same boy became
a *morality policeman,* he rode his motorcycle
through the streets of Tehran cutting women's bared arms
with a poison razorblade.

I Was Sung into This World

I came into this world on the same bed
I later slept in as a child.
My aunt, a midwife, large brown eyes,
scar the shape of the sun on one cheek,
sat at the gate of my mother's womb,
sang me into this world:

Biya koo-choo-loo, Beeya a-zizam
Injah khayli Ghashangeh, Beeya Beeya
Beeya koo-choo-loo, Beeya a-zizam
Noor ast o avaz, eshgh o mah
Beeya Beeya
Ghal-bemoon shokoo-feh kar-deh barayeh tu
Toolesh nadeh
Beeya Beeya   Beeya Beeya   Beeya Beeya

Come little one, come dear one
It's beautiful here, come come
Come little one, come dear one
We've songs, light, a kind moon and love
come come
Hearts here have blossomed to receive you
Don't tarry
come come   come come   come come

It was this song I followed into this world.
Today, yellowed by age and cancer,
my aunt's sapphire wings are spread.
I sit by her bed, make her promise
to come for me when it is my time,
to sing me into the other life
with the same song.

View from Above

The Cross-Eyed Girl

The cross-eyed girl, the one
other children did not befriend
teaches you all about djinn—

How they appear without warning
in steamy bath houses, hooves knocking
the tile floors, so the women—breasts hanging
on stomachs, long black hair limp-wet on their backs—
bite the flesh between thumb and forefinger
                                    —once, twice, three times—
then: *Allah-u-Akbar.*

But she never fears the djinn
because they do not know which eye to look into,
do not know which way to her soul.

The Attack of the Crows

Children are as white sheets. Stain them and they are marked.
—Grandmother

When they shut the *Pious Girls'* school in southern Tehran,
your own school floods with crows. Eyes narrowed,
squeezing out light, they peck the *unbelievers,*
caw-caw: *unclean, unclean.*

Fine black feathers darken the air, invade
the corridors, the classrooms, the cafeteria . . .

Choking little girls
little girls
little girls
like you.

Rain, Rain All Week

The sky's ass has ripped, complains
the neighbor across the street who always sits
on her front steps mending other people's clothes,
spying on all comings and goings.

I want to go to the market for bread and herbs, she moans
holding up a fist to the sky as if all the evil of the world
is woven into its grey and black spongy fabric
and the devil, mad with idleness, squeezes it for fun.

But when the sun slices open a corner,
transforms raindrops into falling lint,
the old woman holds out wrinkled palms, and whispers:
Angels!
        and now
her eyes flood bright, she is laughing,
is the girl she must have been years ago before she was lost
to this city of men, rough hands and veils.

Surgeons

We were surgeons that summer.
We had been mechanics the summer before,
breaking old radios and rusted bicycles
just to put them back together again.

But that summer, the summer Mona disappeared,
we roamed the countryside, scalpels in hand
—razors stolen from our fathers—
trapped lizards, frogs or mice, slit them open
from head to tail, picked their insides with our mothers' tweezers,
examined the entrails with a plastic magnifying glass.
We took meticulous notes—or pretended to.

And at last it was we, the children, who found her
in the woods, beneath green oak leaves and cones.
We were looking for lizards and mice.
At first we didn't know what it was, a dead
animal perhaps, blackened with flies.

Then we saw.
It was she, slit open wide.

Orphanage in Shiraz

Think of children as flower buds:
chrysanthemums, asters, roses, lilies
struggling in the dark.

Descend
cold concrete
steps into the cellar,
axe the shades, release the windows . . .
watch them burst open in the sun.

Tehran Treats

Every day on your way home from school,
you beg your mother for treats.
Hot beets, potatoes roasted on red coals, crunchy
raw almonds, green plums so sour they bite into teeth.

The banana vendor is old, yellow, bent,
and not once do you ask your mother
why his children pick up and lick the banana skins
you carelessly throw into the straw basket by his cart.

Knowing the Food on the Table

> The man who can kill calls you his *joo-joo,* kisses your forehead
> and tucks you in each night.

Great Aunt garlic-and-saffron rubs the venison
your father hunted with the rifle hanging on the wall,
stuffs it with raisins, rice, and toasted almonds . . .

But when your mother has the yard ducks killed,
ducks you chased with palms outstretched,
no hunger can lure you to the table to eat them
stewed in crushed walnuts, sugar and pomegranate sauce.

She Forgot

You were ten, and death was a thief
in the night under your bed.
Each night you'd fall asleep
fearing he'd slide out—
silently, pale Dracula
in fancy black cape—
put a hand on your forehead.
You'd never again
see the goldfish in the pond,
eat pickles, crack pistachios
with your teeth, ride your bicycle
through the alley where the boy
you secretly loved, always passed.

Grandmother said, if anyone
should fear death sleeping
under her bed, it should be she.

If he comes, she cooed,
*point your finger to my room.
I'm ready.*

*Remember, if the mirror shatters,
it's only your reflection that's lost.*

But when she became a lump of flesh,
washed and fed three times a day,
Grandmother forgot her own words—
clenched light and air, held fast
to her sheets, to the bland taste
of creamed chicken spooned into her mouth.

Though angels danced, beckoned:
                    Cross the creek.
her flesh withdrew,
                    shocked by icy cold.

Home

The afternoon sun wears the Persian rug's ruby flowers.

Rain-scented breeze plays with blue cotton drapes.

The black lab, a puddle on the floor.

The boy cuddled in the green couch's arms, reads the Adventures of Sinbad.

The girl tastes Latin words, wrinkles her nose, spits them out.

Grandmother listens, humming a long-forgotten tune.

Rooftops of Tehran

You think you're closer to God on your flat rooftop,
that, like the moon, He can see you standing
alone, small, on its vast emptiness where you are
everything, you're all you know,
you are ten.

But you see through the stories they tell, know
that inside everything is nothing, and inside that
is only God: one giant eye hovering above a city
where beatings, cheating, prayers, songs,
and kindness's shade, all are all one color's shades,
and you . . .

You're just a speck of a girl on this rooftop among many.

Confined

Sometimes, even
the sky's pushing down.

She has no wings, but
she knows flight. She's done it

often in her dreams,
taking off from her rooftop,

flying above a city of mournful songs,
dancing a wingless dance.

Longing

Your uncle has been around the block a few,
each time, a shapely new wife on one arm.

When he speaks of longing, aunts click their tongues,
their husbands grin and wink. "Longing? *Havas*," they say,
(meaning, fleeting fancy), "A legal Don Juan", they say,
(meaning, he weds the ladies he craves.)

Your uncle sighs, says nothing, not because they don't understand
but because outside, flatulent donkeys and cars foul the air,
men hustle for a skewer of kebbab or a bowl of ab-goosht,
women rush about in miniskirts or flimsy chadors, high heels
clicking the sidewalks like tapping rain on tin roofs, distracting
the neighborhood boys, the butcher, the baker, the mullah
who whispers *Masha-allah*, but loudly declaims *Astagh-forallah*.

None of them know the longing he speaks of. How it
can make love to one more tenderly than any other. How it
prods one to get out of bed, wash, dress and go on.

It is the salt in the cheese. The pepper in curry. The honey in baklava.

Ask your uncle, why he needs it—
    and he answers the joy of acquisition lasts but a day.
Ask your uncle how it's done—
    he says when pockets bulge with gold, everything is duck soup.
Ask your uncle, for how long—
    and he smiles, sips his vodka as longing lacquers his hazel eyes.

Shimran Café Adventure

You are twelve.
Your full-bosomed aunt has brought you
to this red velvet draped café.
She has a rendezvous with her "man-friend."

You are both supposed to be out shopping.

She gives you a pen and a ruled journal,
says: *Write a story for me—*
but not about me. She winks,

puts a bowl of ice cream on your table, with hips
swaying, moves towards the man with the Clark Gable
mustache, slicked-back hair, and moss-green eyes.

You want to write about him: that he is in love

with you, and somehow he must break
the news to your poor aunt. Instead,
you watch the man and the woman

framed by pouring window light. You don't know
much about people like them. Your parents never go
to cafés, never hold hands, eye to eye, like that.

The man leans across the table, whispers something,
she flings her head back and laughs like no woman
you have seen. You want to know what he just said.

You want to laugh like that.

Someday, you will break your word and write
a poem about her. But today you eat ice cream.

Middle Eastern Eyebrows

Every time you sink in thought, you pull
your thick eyebrows together, and that makes a frown.

Mother says: *It isn't good for a girl to frown.*
Men can do it, but girls look sour.

But you're not sour. You're thirteen. Happy
when alone with your daydreams.

You put adhesive tape between your brows.
Now you can think and not be sour.

Sweet Sixteen

You are sixteen. First trip to Jerusalem.
Fashionably clothed by London's Harrods—
khaki pants tied at the ankles with silk ribbons,
khaki top with slits for pockets, a khaki beret
placed just so above your long curls that cascade
down your back, and in high heel patent leather shoes,
you are a picture of high fashion, an Iranian girl in London's best
striding proudly into the Tel Aviv airport.

There are stares, furtive smiles, wide-eyed inspections,
every head turned. You think you are *something,*
a modern day beauty unleashed, a future movie star, until you see
you are a stooge dressed like the soldier with the gun.

Secrets

Secrets migrate from the tongue,
the eyes, to the heart—

        steeped in blood, they lose
        their pungent odor of deceit.

Shame

With stolen berries from the neighbor's yard,
you hid in the cold cellar, ate between each kiss,

berry blood staining your clothes.

Look how ink darkens the page,
burdens it with forgotten shadows.

Villages of the Unseen

Ride your rusty bicycle past boundaries
to the villages of the unseen,
of women in chadors, girls hidden
in cellars and kitchens, behind every tall wall,

Ride into the land of dusty roads,
toothless farmers, of mended wash hanging
on ropes, of hookah pipes bubbling,
of women who speak the tongue of grief,

Watch the color of light on mud walls,
on narrow streams where young brides bend
to wash their wares, on mosque doors
mirrored to reflect "faith,"

With the eye of a bird,
hard, bright and wet, watch the men
from among mulberry leaves, wings
flapping, flapping, ready.

Religious Education

In the name of God, he lacerates
with his tongue, parts flesh
sinew by sinew, licks off the blood,
lovingly.

Deepest scars lie beneath
unbroken skin.

The Village Well

You were children, curious. Something splashed
in the belly of the well and she took your hand, descended
into the mouth opened wide,
step by concrete step down its dark spiral throat.

The creature that unhinged the damp stillness
of that well was not a man, not an animal—
just the silhouette of something vast. . . .
You thought it was God, she thought it was djinn,
and then you with fear did not think at all, running back up
breathless, the chill of the well at your heels.

That night you didn't wait for his leg to accidently
rub against yours, or his hand accidentally brush
your thigh as it always did, away from eyes that never
blinked. Instead, you reached for his knee, the flesh and bone
of this gray man who pretended to be daddy's friend. Beneath
the table laden with almond rice your mother had lovingly cooked,
the saffron-stewed lamb, the chicken smothered in herbs . . .
you squeezed,
squeezed so hard his eyes turned your direction and melted
into a watery scream like the one still rising in the throat of that well.

By the Caspian Sea

Three days in a row,
every afternoon
a little girl—
cinnamon,
plays on the sun-polished sand.

Each day she dips her red plastic
watering can into the sea, waters
a pair of men's discarded
sandals, pats them

over and over, as if
she has planted the seed
of another father in those plastic shoes, as if
soon they'll sprout his feet,

(Her parents, blue-eyed
and blonde, speak to her
in a cacophonous foreign tongue,
take turns watching her while
tanning on the beach.)

sprout his body's trunk, the black
flower of his head . . . a man
with tongue honeyed with the melodies of her land
looking on with brown eyes regal as her own.

Suicidal Stars

Each summer you watched shooting stars dive
into the Caspian Sea and wondered why they chose
to leave their heaven home for those cold waters,

gray and full of djinn, where drowned Russian
and Iranian children met. You stood on the soft feather
sand thinking, the sea's so deep it takes in world after world.

Years later, when doctors, professors, and architects fled
Iran to become dishwashers and taxi drivers in a faraway land,
you understood the stars' plight, their plunge, their headlong fall.

Arrival

Just as blue, as silent, as cold
they fished your father out
as they do you now
                                        with icy rods,
                    out from the deeps of your mother,
                                        her eyes fixed
                                    to the soulless lamp.
Her skin is damp. The salt walls press in.
            Her lips' small waves murmur your name.

Your Toes

They speak their great-grandmother's tongue
Remember the soft shoes given them by the Czar

How he sucked on them
Ten nipples, ten erections

Painted henna red
Rubbed with almond oil

Smelling of distant fields
Where she left an infant behind

Azza, The Ceremony of Grief

Women in black, rock
their bodies, beat their chests,
girl-children serve in glass
tumblers steaming auburn tea,
baklava on plastic trays.

Here, tears flow like streams,
wet the ornate Persian rugs
and in the courtyard
            where she poured kerosene on her head, struck a match,
silver fish roam the small pond, oblivious.

On the other side of the yard, men sit
with hookah pipes, crack salted pistachios.

The butcher who was to take the girl as bride
sits on an embroidered cushion, strokes his twisting gray mustache.

At Her Father's Memorial Service

Two hundred people came dressed in black,
dreary grey, muted blue, mouths ballooned
with buttery halva, mumbling: *Oh bless his soul.*

For five years, he steeped in the vinegar of death.

No one came to hold his hand,
place a sprig of jasmine on his chin,
say: *Here, breathe deep. Remember this.*

The Six-Fingered Man

His hands flail the setar strings
as he hunts blindly ancient notes.

And you want to be that setar, long
for surrender's sweet pain,

the sultry strum, the lustful pull,
the giving in to such hands.

Waiting

Hours fall backward.

This earth is but a dot in another world's sky.

She must un-become.

Unhook herself from herself.

Waiting for a wave.

It isn't the guillotine's blade that kills,
the executioner's hand unties the rope.

Her faith is butter melting on hot sand,

waiting for a wave.

When love comes, words fail.
She seeks the one without words.

She waits for a wave.

Awakening

—The Keeper is clever.

You lost your faith
the day the horizon's line
focused into a cage's bar.

Ran towards it,
slashed (no physical marks)
your forehead. The pain
throbs from inside.

View from Above

A figure walks on the beach.
The sun is setting and he is a silhouette,
his shadow walking in front.

From up here, on the bluff,
he makes two identical figures
indistinguishable, deceiving.

Grandmother laughs, slaps your back and points.
Look, she says, *there's God and the Devil*
walking on the sand.

Can you tell me which is which?

The Tulips of Tehran

The Tulips of Tehran

The tulip garden north of the city is in bloom.
From the adjacent ground come the sounds of bickering,
laughter, shouts of children.

In a month, they will all be
dead, the tulips—but now they stand
tall on slim green stalks, flash fancy reds,
pinks and pearls. And the children?

By dusk
they'll be back in their little homes, eating dinner, watching
the country crumble on TV. This is the story of this
garden, not of the children or the war they will soon have to fight.

The children's lives end in the garden's imagination
with the tulip's death.

Censored Poem

The Day the ████ died . . .
the ███ became a man, wore a turban.

Soon bearded angels will ride down on dragon wings,
drag us naughty girls by silky hair, whip us
with leather straps made from Heaven cows.

Daddy's Key

A child in Tehran cries *Daddy!*
out the window at every passing man.
Each morning his mother explains
about the war with Iraq, about the key
to paradise sewn to his father's pants,
but every evening the child forgets,
pushes the window open,
waits . . .

Telephoning a Poet

Enshallah means God willing.

The lines between LA and Tehran
crackle. She laughs, says: *They do this*
on purpose to make us want to hang up.

She is seventy-five, can say what she wants;
calls *them* black monsters in turbans, dark
shrouds clouding the sun above Iran.

Mikham soorat-eto bebinam, you say.
I want to see your face.
She laughs, says: *Soon, soon. We will break bread*

in my house; glasses brimming champagne, we will
dance through the streets of Tehran. Yes,
yes, soon, this Nowruz, when the hyacinths bloom.

You want to believe her.
Enshallah, Enshallah.

Boosh bezoodi dar meeyad, she says. *Soon*
we'll smell what's been brewing.

Enshallah means God willing.

What does God have to do with any of this?

You want to go back—to the land
you remember. They say it doesn't exist.

New Years come and go. Iran elects a president
who pushes poets and women into holes.

The Men, Plural

At night they come in masks and hoods,
in fatigues, in paint, with guns and swords,
machetes, blades, flags of stars,
of stripes, with crosses, with crescents, and skulls,
they march, they sneak, they whisper, they shout
they threaten, they plunge and bust and lunge,
into hearts, into groins, into girls, they come,
they fist, they smack, they grin, they grin.

Stoning the Prostitute

The first and last time your father slapped you,
you were ten.

Angry, fed up with being a child, not heard,
not seen—a girl—you threatened to run away

to *Shahreh-Noe,* the New City, a forbidden place
older girls talked about at school.

That's when your father's large hand, like an angry
tree branch left a mark on your cheek.

You were banished to your room—no dinner, no friends forever,
no breathing the air outside your home, no sun, no moon, nothing.

You didn't know the New City wasn't a city. Didn't know
the ways of women ruled by men, hunger and despair.

Today you saw her picture in the paper . . .
a woman who looks like you.

This is the way of men and large hands.
You, slapped away from harm, she, slapped into it,

her legs forced wide from age eight to eighteen, and now . . .
Let *the sinner* get what she deserves.

Honor

His daughter's room never locked.

His scimitar by the torch light.
Falcate moon shadows the mud wall.

Above her bed, a triptych,
Birth, Birth, Birth,
                    arriving is also leaving.

And the language of surrender
comes from the nectar of breasts.

Her first word was *yes.*

Weep, weep, for God sits with his cohorts.

She is bawdy—even though violated.
She is body, djinn's temptation.

A pomegranate stain never washes out.

Bam

At last,
these men bring lanterns and flashlights:
dig.

In the earth: an infant suckling
his dead mother's breast.
They pull him into the live air.

The dogs refuse to leave.
They stand in the darkening wind
barking at the dirt.

A 6.6 magnitude earthquake struck in southeastern Iran on December 26, 2003, destroying much of the city of Bam. It killed over 43,000 people, injured 20,000, left 60,000 homeless.

After the Tsunami

The women could not outrun
the waves. Those who survived became rare
commodities: kidnapped, raped, forced to marry.

If this were reversed, if
it had been men swallowed by waves, if
women outnumbered men . . .

once again, women would be forced to marry—
many wives to each man.

This is the world.

This is why you hide your wings.   You don't want them bitten off.

His Parents "Disappeared" in the Suburbs of Tehran

It's an image on your computer screen.
He stands in a garden, dressed in black.
No coffins because no bodies were found.
Disappeared, said the man behind the steel desk.

You trace your friend's tears
with the blinking cursor on your screen,
wondering if this is how
God chooses to touch us all.

"Endless Love," Islamic Revolutionary Style

The gold label reads: *Coming to you from Victoria's secret garden,*
as if picked from a soft-shell pistachio tree in a sultan's grove.

The label insists, if used in liberal amount
skin transforms to *petal soft, wonderfully fragrant.*

It claims primrose oil and chamomile,
promises to *smooth on easily, absorb quickly,*
urges to *lavishly smooth over damp skin after shower or bath.*

So she runs herself a bath, soaks as prescribed:
towel dries, lifts up the bottle, squirts,
spares no parts—neck, arms, stomach, and beyond.

Then, slips into a crimson strapless gown, a pair of red velvet shoes,
pulls a black *chador* over her head . . .

And off she goes to a party on the corner of Imam
Holy Avenue and the Alley of the Pious.

Eternal Prayer

Easy to be bored in Saudi Arabia, he says.
Not much to do for a stranger.

He gets in a company car, asks a man
pulling on a camel, *Which way the desert?*

The man looks into his eyes, points to the east,
then the west, says: *Go with Allah, He is everywhere.*

He glides towards the sun and the sun
towards him until there is nothing but sand.

He bows and lays down his head.

History Lesson

Listen,

when bombers,

penetrating clouds,

release their sperm

to red-wash the earth,

when love

is a soil-trapped seed,

tie yourself to a tree,

cover yourself with leaves—

this too shall never pass.

Going Back to Iran

You will one day go back, rub
your cheek against your old house door.
Will it remember the child, click wide
its wooden jaws, or creak shut, slam, betray?

And if it opens its timber arms,
will it embrace her with hinges' moans,
order the windows to attention,
chandeliers to high alert?

No Apple Trees in This Paradise

Morning After the U.S. Invasion of Iraq

It is as it has always been in Redlands.

At GFE on the corner of Cajon and Vine
people suck coffee from paper cups,
munch on muffins from Martha Green's Bakery.

The chatter is as always, quiet.
The smiles as always, broad.

But today the sun is concealed and the breeze
brings no news of the orange grove
down the road in Prospect Park.

Perhaps last night trees shed blossoms like sap
—trees grieve like that.

The Wall

She takes a nail, places it on the spot she has marked,
bites her upper lip, lifts the hammer, misses with a loud crash.

This is my cousin, the one with the Lucille Ball face,
black hair, unbroken eyes. She wants to hang her dead
husband's picture on the wall.

The large hole in the paper-thin wall scares her stiff
as does the thought of her priggish landlord with his pinkish eyes,
the grey hair jutting out his pockmarked nose.

It's been only a month since she arrived in London,
a lone woman, two children in tow, little money,
open wide for what may come—work, luck, anything.

And now she is terrified because this will not do, this large hole
in the wall for which the landlord could kick her out
with no pity in his gurgling kidney pie-fed gut.

She hurries to Harry's hardware where just last week
she bought two plastic chairs, grabs old Harry's sleeve,
and in fearless broken English cries, *I have a big hole. Too big.*
I want make it smaller. You help?

Harry laughs and calls over Joe, who calls over Mike,
and they consult, their bald heads together, three chuckling
chums. They send her to the shop two doors down,

and my cousin, the sight of the big hole in the wall still patched to
her mind's eye, stumbles into the red-shaded shop, is startled
by a woman screaming, *Yes, yes, give it to me baby. You're the king.*

She looks up at the glaring screen, sees that the one addressed
with such ardor is no Shah, just a balding naked man
convulsing like one possessed, over a woman's pale body.

The shop sells unspeakable things, but the one that catches her eye
uncannily resembles her dead husband's private part. She knows where
this is. A practical joke on a foreign woman with a broken tongue.

Still, she needs to mend her wall, not be kicked out, eke, survive.
She catapults out of the sex shop and back into Harry's Hardware,
her chin not down, her eyes not averted, her shoulders not sagged.

With flames roasting her cinnamon eyes, burning her bony cheeks,
my cousin politely asks: *You help me. I have a hole*
in the wall. The wall.

Step Out

Stop when you stop Mehrullah
in the airport.
Stop when you stop Ziba-Talab.

What's in a name? Meaning?
Mehrullah means love of God.
Ziba-Talab is one who craves beauty.

And look, John Crotch just went by.
Stop him!
His name is all bathroom talk.

Do you know the story of the land of Ta, where
the sun burned blue, turned human skin milky white?
The sun-starved of the land were as dark as night.

The Photograph

It is large, square, black and white.
A happy picture. A father, an uncle, a sheik
and an Imam—head wrapped in a turban,
a long *aba* draped across his shoulders, silver
wire glasses on the tip of his nose. He is smiling.
They're all smiling, the four kind-faced men.

The men are looking down at the little girl, Noor,
three years old, dark eyes, long eyelashes. But
Noor is looking away at something far past the edge
of the photograph, perhaps lost in a childhood daydream: running
on a wind-caught beach in a pink swimsuit, blue glitter in front. Yet, here
her body stands small, covered in black cloth, not a strand of hair
visible, no arms, knees, only the smooth skin of her face and hands.

Towering above her, four good men, pleased
with little Noor. They, in their short-sleeve shirts
in Chicago's mid-summer heat.

In the End What Folly

In an abandoned elementary school
a priest baptizes marines in a makeshift pond
brimming with canteen water.

Purified, the young soldiers can hope for paradise.

Outside, bearded men answer the noon prayer call,
rest guns against battered walls, turn to Mecca,
bow, hands on knees, before merciful Allah.

Prayer-purified, they too wish for paradise.

And in the end what folly,
(oh God of gods, what folly)
takes them all to a sunless, dreamless land?

No Apple Trees in This Paradise

The newscaster on the radio
speaks of empty streets in Iraq
except for the dance of gunmen.

With the tip of my manicured finger
I quiet her and let the caws of crows
in the garden hold sway.

Our street in Redlands is empty
except for the white rabbits' mad dash
across the peony-bordered road.

To protect our paradise
we have outsourced our sins
to hells we help daily create.

There is a serpent in my garden
but I tell it I have no apple trees.
Here, we only grow blood oranges.

And So It Goes . . .

In the dusty market beneath makeshift canopies,
bodies captive in Baghdad's summer heat,
she tugs on her mother's *chador*, holds up a copper coin
in her tiny palm, asks *where to buy bombs to attack the Americans.*

My child cousin often marched around the round
mahogany table, fist punching air, chanting:
Marg bar Shah. Death to the Shah.

Months later, the Shah fled Iran.

Drought-empowered beetles, hungry,
killed countless old pines in San Bernardino mountains.
Then came the fire,
ruthless, sweeping . . .

Holy Water

At a party for a man who is now
a woman living with a lesbian lover,
the butterball woman sitting next to me on the couch
tells me she had her dog blessed

at a Catholic church in Hollywood.
She says there was an ad in the paper.
People brought their birds, cats, lizards,
even fish, to be blessed by holy water.

I ask her if she is Catholic.
Oh no, I'm Jewish, she says.
But I wanted my dog blessed.

This reminds me of Mashad-reezeh, how its *Kad-khoda,*
the village chief, always rose at the crack of dawn
to pray, performing ablutions with cloudy pond water,
thick with moss, fish feces, and drowned stars.

The Outsider

I know what it's like to be an outsider, a *kharejee.*

I know how English sounds
when every word is only music.

I know how it feels not
to be an American, an English, a French.
Call them
            —*Amrikayee, Ingleesee, Faransavi,*
see them
            see me as alien, immigrant, *Iranee.*

But I've been here so long.
they may call me American,
      with an American husband
      and American children . . .

But mark this—I do not belong anywhere.
I have an accent in every language I speak.

Moral America

At the radio station
the host warns, "Remember,
no offensive words like fuck,
penis or vagina," and we go on
the air with words like rape,
genocide and torture.

At Reno Airport

A wide-shouldered guard greets me and I quickly
greet her back, move on because I'm from the Middle East
and you just never know.

But the white-blue uniform follows,
watches me order a sandwich,
sit in a corner with my book.

Hell, I think, *damn my thick eyebrows.*
She's on to me. I carry tweezers
and those pluckers are sharp, can be held
against the delicate white throat of a flight attendant
for an extra bag of peanuts or a can of diet coke.

The guard approaches and I almost choke on my BLT,
trying to remember in which pocket of my bag
I have tossed the deadly weapon.

I was at your reading last night, she says so loud
the passengers around, nervous until now, turn
their heads to look at my face. *You write sad things,*
but also funny. Loved the poem about your brother
at the Canadian border. I bought two books, gave one to my friend.
Her smile is a row of perfect melon seeds.

She thanks me for coming to Reno, snow
and slot machines, then brings her wide face close,
whispers: *I have to go now. I'm supposed to take things away
from people. It's my job.* She giggles and suddenly she is not
as she was before. Just a girl.

The man at the next table walks to the counter,
picks up paper napkins, and I watch him because I need
some too. On his way back he lays a few on my table, nods,
goes back to his hamburger, coke and fries.

Los Angeles, 2007

I'm sitting at the Starbucks on the corner
of 11th and Grand drinking my daily triple
espresso macchiato, reading the LA Times,
when a truck, lined with mirrors, stops
at the red light and I see my reflection in a world
where I seem at ease, the sun lounging on bare
shoulders, the breeze weaving through dark curls,
and my delicate long Indian print skirt elegantly
spread about my ankles. I look coyly amused, as if
I'm reading a cheesy romance in which the dashing,
muscular, half-naked hero rides his stallion through
daisy-dotted green hills towards the hut where his
beloved waits, her heaving sighs threatening to pop
her ample bosom out from a busty saffron gown.

But the truth is that I'm reading about a possible U.S. attack on a country
I still call home, and I'm sobbing inside, not for the bozos who cultivate
facial hair instead of compassion and grace, but for my friends, my old
neighbors, people who create, cook, clean and clamor for a living, people
who laugh, love, and lollygag, just like we do, yes, you and me.

Inside despair, I cry.

Last night when my gentle friend drove like a madman
getting us that much closer to death because the tattooed
giant in the large black SUV was rude and fast, or when
my friend's husband, who marches in peace rallies, places

a pillow on her delicate face one night, his eyes crimson
with booze and rage, or when a patron of the arts surprises
me with: *I consider you one of us,* meaning white, I wonder
if there is hope for any of us after all.

The traffic light turns green and the mirror-lined truck moves on, takes
with it the serene, dream-soft woman in the long, flowing skirt.

The Deep Dive

Stevie's raisin-colored braids,
a shade lighter than his skin,
bob up-down as the waves punch the boat.

He signals *Go down.*
I don't.

I stay close to the boat,
hold tight the taut rope.
                                        Can't breathe.
Not the air in the tank.
Not the air in the air.
My lungs inflate, deflate,
but that's beside the point.
                                        I can't fuckin' breathe,
and I yell this to the waves,
to the boat,
to Stevie
who magically surfaces beside me,
an aurous brown god in goggles,
regulator hose dangling by his mouth.
He holds my head between his palms, says,
                                        "But you ARE breathing. You ARE."

I look at him and even in this panic, this feeling
of imminent death, I note how beautiful he is,
how I could perhaps outlive this storm

in this man's brawny arms, let myself go
and the hell with the world,
with who I am, or am supposed to be,
with my anxious lover waiting at the shore.

"Relax, baby," says Stevie, "I'll stay with you."
He pulls me into his arms and I breathe deep
from the tank strapped to my back. Stealthily
he releases air from my jacket, adds
a cube of weight to my belt,
and down we go, down
into the broth of another world.

The sea bottom is a sandy desert flush against massive rocks,
and there are cacti, tiny Joshua trees, and brown grass dancing
to the water current's silent tango . . .
Time means nothing here.
Palestine, Israel, and Tehran mean nothing here,
my daughter contemplating suicide at twelve means nothing here,
sons in military fatigue breathing Iraqi air means nothing here,
even women giving life and grenades taking them away,
mean nothing here.

Here, the fish are birds,
electric blue fins, wings,
and beneath this airless sky, Stevie and I.

Defiance

Naked

Delicious sleeping naked between
soft cotton sheets as licking
velvety gelato or dipping
a finger in milky puffs of cream.

The birds know this.
Know the air's downy lithe
dip of wings into ghostly clouds.
Here, take my hand. This is how.

Weed Killer

> *Atrazine, a top selling weed killer in the United States and the world, has been found to (seep into ponds and as a result to) dramatically affect the sexual development of male frogs, turning them into hermaphrodites.*
>
> —*National Geographic News*

Let's all drink the water,
wear soft shimmering dresses,
get pedicures, wear mascara and perfume,
turn battered-women shelters into dance halls.

God will be soft, plump and warm,
her words flowing like poetry
not from atop a cold gold throne
but from fields of sweet peas, dandelions and wild rose.

Let's all drink from the pond,
become witches and witch-dance for the moon,
cuddle under sheets embroidered pink,
smash all anorexic mannequins in the stores.

No more quaking snores, grunts,
bed-shattering masculine farts,
thick hair jutting out from ears and nose.
Let's unstitch genitals and lips.

Let's all drink from the pond,
bury the guns, the swords, the patterned boxer shorts.
Put soldiers in high heels so they can't run
let their nails grow long so they won't pull triggers

as blood deserts their shrinking penises
and pumps into their ever-swelling hearts.

The Appointment

One o'clock sharp,
he shows up at my door, blue jeans,
red work-shirt, his blonde hair
messy curly about his face.
Big smile, says: *At your service.*

I invite him in, tell him to take off
his shoes, lead him upstairs.
He bends over it,
tenderly,
whips out his snake
long, longer
shoves it in, looks at me
says: *Satisfaction guaranteed.*

Afterwards, we go outside,
he smokes a cigarette, I
write him a check.

You need a new one, he says.
I've field-tested many, and
your toilet is no good.

He smiles, flashes uneven teeth.
They are yellow, like his hair.

Max Ernst's "*A Hundred Thousand Doves*"

He couldn't know where they came from,
these paint birds he scraped into flight,
just as he couldn't have known

we would stand before the riot, lips on lips
groins touching, not seeing the doves, but riding them

into colors—away from the watchful guard . . .

Bees

The tattoo on the girl's stomach:
a swarm of bees rushing
up from beneath her pants
as if from a nest inside—
dark, moist and warm
where they breed, feeding
on lovers' nectar.
Here's one now—a lover—holding
her hand, whispering in her hair.

She is young.

Perhaps in twenty years she'll
walk this same beach alone,
the swarm of bees up to her chin.

Walking in the Woods

The leaves like spry spirits
rush me and who's to say if
the wind is their God,
that any other force but their own bright will
is responsible for their merry, careless dance?

Even the dust on my boots,
excited, rises—
                    pirouettes into the autumn air.

That Desire Called Sin

after Forugh Farrokhzad

Naked, you climb the boulder with a flashlight and mother's
painted bowl brimming with cherries.
You whisper to the moon, *I must be mad.*

You've come to wash away your sins, but the creek giggles,
runs watery hands on your thighs as Venus stares, spreads
her molten blue beams on your hair.

The cherries explode red in your mouth and you spit out the seeds
as if each is a planet crusted with guilt, swallow the soft flesh
murmuring, *nothing's more delectable than sin.*

If Only We Could Hear Fish Sing

The California blonde roasting in the sun

Wants to be the color of the girl south of the border.

The girl south of the border dyes her hair blonde.

Soon we will all look like one another.

If we could hear fish sing

there would be peace on earth.

Axing the Horses

Axing the Horses

Faith is a fire my parents fuel and fan to keep us warm against the fanaticism that has brought on the winter outside our walls. It is a sharp-dry warmth that chaps our lips, and makes us itch all over. We are told for everything good one must suffer. The sky outside our triple-paned windows is smoky grey. I don't know if the glass is tinted and I know no other windows to compare them to.

Hawks whirl in the sky's belly looking for prey, and below in the streets, crows hop about crapping, gossiping, looking for sinners to peck. I am told I must fear these crows and hawks, their beady eyes, tiny brains, their sharp beaks and claws. Each time I go out I must bow in prayer three times then armor myself with a shield of lead, and a kind smile just to show the goodness of my heart, the brightness of my soul. Yet, I am allowed no friends from the dusty, grimy world outside. I sometimes sneak out, but guilt is a barbed chain that always pulls me back in. I begin to obediently stay within the confines of our walls and soon I only see crows and hawks. The nightingales and their uninhibited songs, the delicate bodies of the hummingbirds, the swish of their wings, their incessant search for nectar, all begin to disappear from my memory like the sweetness of candy that slowly dissolves on the tongue and imperceptibly vanishes from the senses.

One day, quite accidentally, when I go up to the flat rooftop of our house to fetch sour cherry syrup to sweeten my aunt's water, I see a shooting star. Why is it running so fast? Who and what is it running from? I look at the other stars and see that they are as still as they have always been, firmly planted on the blue-black face of the sky. That night my sleep fills with shooting stars. *Where are you going?* They do not stop to answer. They vanish and the suddenly starless sky begins to weep snow.

I continue, every night, to chase the shooting stars, those fisted balls of fire, asking, asking, asking . . . but no answers. My skin turns blue. Dark circles hang under my eyes. No one notices. Only I can see my gradual decay in the mirror that occupies my room. *I am the sky and I'm losing my stars,* I murmur to my fading image.

One evening it snows and snows and I mumble something about no stars in the sky. Father says it is because they are obscured by the clouds. But I know better. The sky is weeping and that means something strange is about to happen . . . and something strange does happen, in the form of an invitation to an amusement park. The park is lit up and loud. Father and mother hold my hands tighter than usual lest I slip away and be carried off by the river of men and women whose blood is not red. We, family, walk about, all senses alert. Then I see it—the merry-go-round, its large wooden horses, their heads held high as if ecstatic, the way my girlfriend and I sometimes do when we dial random numbers—casting a line into the waters outside our walls to see if we'd catch a fish. If we do, our voices drowning, we quickly hang up the phone—that is, throw him back into the water. No harm done. No sin committed.

I pull on my parents hands and lead them toward the glittering merry-go-round alive with music. My brothers follow as we step onto the platform. Father sits on a large black steed, the whites of its eyes larger than its painted irises. Mother chooses a pony . . . one she imagines she can manage. Brothers each hop on silver horses, as if they are TV cowboys. I stand on the platform, hold on to a brass pole. I laugh because the horses are made of wood. I'm not interested in their painted hooves, their stiff mains, their veneered bodies. No, I'm interested in the ride, the spin, the whirling. I want to see the park, the world as we spin. I want to feel the movement, the going. As the organ music starts to play and the platform begins to spin, slowly, then fast, faster, I watch the landscape go around and around until everything is a shooting star—the men, women, the fences, dogs, the lights . . .

How to stop it all? Spinning, I finally understand. Understand the aromatic tainted nectar fed me through my mother's breasts, the dry sinless warmth of my house, the shield of lead, the tainted windows, the high cement walls. It isn't that the stars are running away. It is me moving around and around. I howl. I laugh and clap my hands. I look at my family so taken with the wooden horses. To them, these creatures are alive and this is life, this spinning platform, its horses made of dead trees, and this unchanging mediocre music.

An axe hangs next to a red handle covered with glass. High on my light-flooded madness, I grab it and swing at the horses. Father rushes towards me. Mother screams. I leap off the spinning platform falling on my back to a sweet kind of death. Finally free, the hawk and crow feathers float about like snow shadows. Ah yes, there is life after such death. Its air is scented with jasmine, its sky filled with stars. I know, outside our walls, it has always been winter, but here it is summer, my eternal summer. I point to on my skin glowing, tell them: *Look! I'm bathed in light.*

No, mother says from behind the wall. *That's the Beloved leaving your soul.*

Vocabulary

Ab-goosht—Hearty lamb stew cooked with legumes, tomato paste, potatoes and spices. A common dish among Iranian peasants.

Allah-u-Akbar—God is great.

Astagh-forallah May God forbid; May God forgive.

Azza—Mourning for the dead.

Aba—A long cape worn by Muslim ecclesiastes.

Chador—Long, loose piece of cloth worn by women to cover themselves. A pious woman's chador is opaque and black, but chadors before the 1979 revolution in Iran came in many colors and transparencies.

Djinn—In Muslim mythology: spirits, lower than the angels, capable of appearing in human and animal forms.

Ensha-allah—God willing.

Kadkhoda—Village headman.

Kharejee—Foreigner; Outsider.

Masha-allah—What wonders God hath wrought!

Nowruz—The Iranian New Year.

Setar—An Iranian musical instrument. A member of the lute family. Not to be confused with the Indian Sitar.

Shareh-Noe—Tehran's red light district.

Shimran—A posh neighborhood in northern Tehran.

References and Comments

"And So It Goes"—Line 4 quotes from The Los Angeles Times, May 29, 2004

"The Tulips of Tehran" and "Daddy's Key"—Iran-Iraq war began shortly after the 1979 revolution and lasted eight years (1980-1988). Saddam Hussein was provided weapons and support by the United States throughout those years. Iranian children were often recruited by the Islamic Republic of Iran to run ahead of the soldiers in order to clear out the mine fields. Each child and soldier was provided with a key to Heaven.

"Telephoning a Poet"—Based on an actual conversation with a poet residing in Iran. Initially I named her in the title of the poem, but later, fearing for her safety, I replaced her name with "a poet."

"Stoning the Prostitute"—Though stoning women is not common practice in Iran, nonetheless it does take place in smaller towns and hamlets. These women are not protected by law.

"His Parents 'Disappeared' in the Suburbs of Tehran"—During the first few years of the 1979 Iranian revolution, many men and women systematically and mysteriously "disappeared." These were people the government deemed "threatening" to the government they were establishing. Later, the established government no longer conducted these eradications clandestinely. Many innocent people were executed openly as infidels or traitors and the cost of bullets were often demanded from the victims' families.